Untethered: 30 Days of Pressing on in Hope in Obedience

A Devotional Journey Toward Faith, Obedience, and Peace

Raychel Shaw

Copyright © 2025 Steps of Obedience Press

All rights reserved.

ISBN: 978-8-9897040-5-7

DEDICATION

To God alone be the glory and honor forever and ever

ACKNOWLEDGMENT

Scripture quotations taken from the Holy Bible, New International Version®, NIV®. Copyright © 1973, 1978, 1984, 2011 by Biblica, Inc.™ Used by permission. All rights reserved worldwide.

Scripture quotations taken from the New American Standard Bible®, NASB®. Copyright © 1960, 1962, 1963, 1968, 1971, 1972, 1973, 1975, 1977, 1995 by The Lockman Foundation. Used by permission. www.Lockman.org

Scripture quotations are from The Holy Bible, English Standard Version® (ESV®), copyright © 2001 by Crossway, a publishing ministry of Good News Publishers. Used by permission. All rights reserved.

Scripture quotations taken from the New King James Version®. Copyright © 1982 by Thomas Nelson. Used by permission. All rights reserved

CONTENTS

Section 1 – Being Untethered (Days 1–7)
Raw, honest, "in the thick of it" reflections that immediately connect with readers who feel untethered.

Section 2 – Wrestling & Refining (Days 8–14)
Devotionals about identity, faith struggles, obedience, and personal growth in hard places.

Section 3 – Anchoring to Truth (Days 15–22)
Encouragement for holding to God's promises and being obedient while still in the tension.

Section 4 – Walking in Hope (Days 23–30)
Strength and clarity for the way forward.

Section 1 – Being Untethered (Days 1–7)

Day 1 – Untethered

Scripture: "We have this hope as an anchor for the soul, firm and secure." – Hebrews 6:19a (NIV)

Supporting Scripture: "Trust in the Lord with all your heart and lean not on your own understanding; in all your ways submit to Him, and He will make your paths straight." – Proverbs 3:5–6 (NIV)

Devotional:

In January 2022, my family and I stepped into what we believed would be a new adventure in a fresh season of calling. It was that — and much more. The "much more" was what I hadn't anticipated.

Shaun and I had built our life in Texas: 22 years of marriage, three amazing kids (plus bonus kids), deep community ties, years of ministry, and even my own business as a certified firearms instructor. We were known. We belonged. Then God called us to go — first to Indiana, then to Virginia — and I felt as though part of me had been ripped away.

In Indiana, the snow melted along with our excitement. I grieved our son staying behind, the loss of our ministry family, and the small comforts of familiarity. Then Virginia brought its own set of challenges: no community, no recognition, and restrictions that felt foreign. I could see God expanding Shaun's influence, but I felt invisible, unsure of my purpose.

That untethered feeling was less like a hot air balloon that has a modicum of control and more like a helium balloon, released from a child's grasp into the wind. I battled depression and even wished for Heaven—not out of a desire to end my life, but because I longed for the perfection of God's presence.

Yet, in the untethering, I learned something: becoming untethered from what I knew tethered me fully to Him. I still don't have all the answers about my purpose in this season, but I trust God's goodness, His leading, and His call to love Him and love others. If sharing my story encourages even one person to keep going, that's enough.

Reflection Questions:

Have you ever experienced a season where God untethered you from something familiar? How did it feel?

What "comforts of familiarity" might you be holding onto instead of holding tightly to God?

How might being untethered actually be an invitation to trust Him more deeply?

Prayer: Lord, when You move me into the unknown, help me trust that You are still my anchor. Remind me that even when I feel adrift, You have not lost hold of me. Use every untethered season to draw me closer to You. Amen.

Day 2 – Untethered & Loved

Scripture: "To Him who loves us and released us from our sins by His blood." – Revelation 1:5b (NASB95)

Devotional:

In The Help, there's a line that has always stuck with me: "You is kind. You is smart. You is important."

Those words were spoken from a place of deep love — not earned, just given. And yet, as we grow older, life and society affected by living in a fallen and broken world that Satan runs amok in can twist our thinking. Love can start to feel like it's tied to our performance.

I remember as a girl feeling like my parents loved me more if I made straight A's or earned first chair in band. Now, as a mom, I know better, because I love my kids no matter what they do — even when I don't love their choices. I remind them often, "There's nothing you could ever do or say to make me not love you."

Still, I've fallen into the trap of measuring my worth by the approval of others. Social media makes it worse, training us to seek validation in likes and comments. That need for external approval warps how we receive feedback and can leave us feeling rejected and unloved.

Recently, during a Bible study on Revelation, we read: "To Him who loves us and released us from our sins by His blood" (Revelation 1:5). Two words stood out to me: loves (continual). Often, I don't feel worth loving — yet here is Jesus, knowing every detail, every sin that he died to release(second word) me from, still loving me, still wanting a relationship with me.

Romans 8:1 says, "There is now no condemnation for those who are in Christ Jesus." This is the truth I must tether myself to — not the opinions of others, not even my own negative thoughts. When I anchor to God's Word instead of the world's (Satan's) lies, I find the courage to live untethered from fear and fully tethered to Jesus.

Reflection Questions:

When have you felt most loved without having to earn it?

What lies or voices try to convince you you're unlovable?

Which Scripture can you cling to when your feelings say otherwise? Hint: In the first chapter of Ephesians God through Paul has a lot to say about who you are in Christ. Underline those words.

Here's my list: Chose(chosen) Holy, blameless, adopted, BELOVED, redemption(redeemed), forgiveness,

Prayer: Lord, thank You for loving me without condition and for releasing me from my sins through Your death, burial, and resurrection. Help me to anchor my identity in what You say about me, not in the opinions of others or the lies of the enemy. Amen.

Day 3 – Fear of the Unknown

Primary Scripture: "But the Helper, the Holy Spirit, whom the Father will send in My name, He will teach you all things, and bring to your remembrance all that I said to you." – John 14:26 (NASB95)

Supporting Scripture: "For God has not given us a spirit of fear, but of power and love and discipline." – 2 Timothy 1:7 (NASB95)

Devotional:

I've always felt a major sense of trepidation when encountering things I know little about or am unfamiliar with. Sometimes I avoid the situation entirely, and other times I prepare myself in advance — like checking a restaurant's menu online before ever walking through the door.

Fear of the unknown isn't just my struggle. As a firearms instructor for over ten years, I've met many people terrified of firearms, often avoiding them at all costs. But when I taught them the parts, functions, and safe handling, something shifted. I could see their shoulders relax as they realized their fear had less to do with the firearm itself and more to do with their lack of understanding.

I realized I had my own "firearm" moment — but with a book of the Bible: Revelation. Even after seminary, I avoided it. I told myself there were 65 other books I understood better, so this one could wait. But if I truly believe the entire Bible is the inspired, authoritative Word of God, I can't skip a part of it just because it feels intimidating.

Through a Bible study called Blessed by Nancy Guthrie, God changed my perspective. Now I think of Revelation not as "apocalypse" but as "reveal." It reveals Jesus — who He is now, before His return — and it brings comfort, not fear. For someone who battles anxiety and depression, that shift is priceless.

Fear shrinks when knowledge grows, especially knowledge rooted in God's Word. Don't let fear of the unknown keep you from what God wants to show you.

Reflection Questions:

What's one area of your life you've been avoiding because it feels unfamiliar or intimidating?

How has God used understanding to replace fear in your past?

Is there a part of God's Word you've avoided that you could start exploring today?

Prayer: Lord, thank You for revealing Yourself through all of Scripture. Replace my fear of the unknown with confidence in Your truth. Teach me by Your Spirit, and help me to face new things with courage and trust in You. Amen.

Day 4 – Comfort

Primary Scripture: "Do not be afraid; I am the first and the last, and the Living One; and I was dead, and behold, I am alive forevermore, and I have the keys of death and of Hades." – Revelation 1:17b–18 (NASB95)

Supporting Scripture: "Therefore, since we have a great high priest who has passed through the heavens, Jesus the Son of God, let's hold firmly to our confession." – Hebrews 4:14 (NASB95)

Devotional:

One of the coolest things I've gotten to see this past year was Niagara Falls. We explored both the Canadian and American sides, and no matter where you stand, the roar of that much water is unmistakable, powerful, and demands respect. After seeing it, I could hear that roar from our hotel at night and know exactly what it was.

While studying Revelation, before Nancy Guthrie even mentioned it, John's description of Jesus' voice in Revelation 1:15 had me thinking the same thing — unmistakable, powerful, worthy of awe — just like Niagara Falls. Jesus says in John 10:27 that His sheep know His voice. It's like my first night at Niagara when I didn't know what I was hearing, but after the encounter, I recognized it instantly.

Here's the thing: I had some definite presuppositions about Jesus. I often picture Him as the humble, meek servant from the Gospels — and He is that — but Revelation 1 shows so much more. High priestly garments. The golden sash of a King. Hair white as snow, just like Daniel's description of the Ancient of Days. The Bible's internal consistency blows me away — from Exodus' detailed priestly garments to Hebrews' declaration that Jesus is our Great High Priest and final sacrifice. It's like those "as seen on TV" commercials — BUT WAIT, THERE'S MORE!

And then there's John's reaction. Back in John 13:23, he's casually reclining next to Jesus. They were close friends! But here? John sees the resurrected King and falls on his face as if dead. And Jesus — loving, powerful Jesus — reaches out His right hand and says, "Do not be afraid. I am the first and the last… I have the keys of death and of Hades."

Whoa! Can you imagine!? The One with all authority over life and death is telling you not to be afraid. That's comfort. That's security. No one leaves this world too early or outside of His timing. The One holding the keys isn't surprised by the when or the how.

I find so much comfort in untethering myself from my presuppositions and tethering myself to the truth of God's Word — to our Savior and King, Jesus Christ, who holds the keys.

Reflection Questions:

How does seeing Jesus as both Savior and reigning King change the way you relate to Him?

What presuppositions about Jesus might you need to untether from to see Him more clearly?

How does knowing Jesus holds the keys of life and death bring you comfort?

Prayer: Lord, thank You for revealing Yourself as both Savior and King. Help me to let go of my limited views of who You are and anchor myself in the truth of Your Word. Thank You that my life is in Your hands, and that I can trust You completely. Amen.

Day 5 – Untethered Obedience

Primary Scripture: "Do you not know that those who run in a race all run, but only one receives the prize? Run in such a way that you may win." – 1 Corinthians 9:24 (NASB95)

Supporting Scripture: "If you love me, keep my commands." – John 14:15 (NIV)

Devotional:

Several years ago, my husband discovered Inky Johnson's testimony, and it was so powerful we showed it to our youth group. We quote Inky a lot, but one of my favorites is his view on commitment. He shared Orebela Gbenga's definition:

"Commitment means staying loyal to what you said you were going to do long after the mood you said it in has left you."

Oof. That one hits me. Think about your exercise plan. The "me" who makes it at 9 p.m. is not the same "me" who wakes up to execute it at 6 a.m. The evening me is feeling it. The morning me? Not so much.

Faith can be like that, especially when seasons change. When God moved us from our last season into this one, part of me was excited for the adventure — but another part was anxious and not thrilled about all the changes that came with it. I remember one of Shaun's teammates asking, "Are you ready for this?" and my reply was, "I don't always agree with God, but I do always have to be obedient to Him."

We prayed over this decision, and while I knew it would be difficult, Shaun was certain God was leading us. So, as the spiritual head of our home, I trusted him, and together we trusted God. That obedience has brought some incredible blessings — and also some really tough, really not-so-good, very bad days with more tears than I can count.

That's when commitment gets tested. Some days you have to choo-choo on and let obedience be the engine while your feelings ride in the caboose. I don't always "feel" like obeying. Sometimes I'm tired, hurt, or just plain lazy. But obedience means following God with the same commitment on the hard days as on the days when everything's going right.

Paul compared obedience to running a race in 1 Corinthians 9:24–27. Runners don't just roll out of bed and win marathons — they train. They're disciplined. They run on the days they don't feel like it so they can finish well. That's the call for us too: untether from feelings and tether yourself to the commitment you made to Christ. Keep running your race.

Reflection Questions:

What commitments to God have been hardest to keep when the "mood" wore off?

How can you prepare yourself spiritually for the "I don't feel like it" days?

What does "letting obedience be the engine and feelings the caboose" look like in your life?

Prayer: Lord, help me to obey You even when my feelings don't line up. Teach me to train my heart in faithfulness and to run my race with endurance. Thank You for the strength to keep going when I'd rather quit. Amen.

Day 6 – Living Untethered from Regret

Primary Scripture: "So, whether you eat or drink, or whatever you do, do all for the glory of God." – 1 Corinthians 10:31 (NASB95)

Supporting Scriptures:

"Keep your tongue from evil and your lips from telling lies; turn from evil and do good; seek peace and pursue it." – Psalm 34:13–14 (NIV)

"Therefore we are ambassadors for Christ, as though God were making an appeal through us…" – 2 Corinthians 5:20a (NASB95)

"If we confess our sins, He is faithful and righteous, so that He will forgive us our sins and cleanse us from all unrighteousness." – 1 John 1:9 (NASB95)

Devotional:

I've never actually seen the movie, but I've seen the clip where Jennifer Aniston's daughter brings home a guy with a giant tattoo across his chest that says "NO RAGRETS." The dad stares at him and says, "You have no regrets? Not even one little letter?" For some reason, I find that hysterical, and it gets quoted around here more often than you'd think.

But let's be honest — we all have regrets. We've all said something we wish we hadn't, made choices that still make us cringe, or taken actions that left ripples we never intended. Sometimes those memories pop up out of nowhere — in the shower, on a sunny walk, or while riding a horse — and suddenly you're replaying moments you'd rather forget.

For me, one of those memories comes from junior high or early high school. I was with a group of kids, desperate to fit in, and I started telling filthy jokes I'd overheard from adults. I used words I'd never normally say, all in an effort to be "one of them." In that moment, I didn't realize I was shaping their mental model of who I was — and it was nothing like who I actually was inside. Today, the memory makes me wince.

I've always had a strong desire to belong. Add in a lifetime of moving around and feeling like an outsider, and it's no wonder I sometimes compromised my character just to be accepted. But here's the truth: what we say, what we do, and even what we choose not to say or do matters. Not just for our reputation's sake, but because as Christians, we're ambassadors for Christ (2 Corinthians 5:20). We carry His name into every situation — whether we're at work, at school, in our living rooms, scrolling on our phones, or walking into church.

I wish someone had told my younger self that my words and actions were shaping not only how others saw me, but how others saw Him. Representing Christ well isn't a Sunday-only thing. It's an all-day, every-day calling. And yes — it matters.

Do I still have regrets? Absolutely. But because of Jesus, I can live untethered to the weight of those regrets. When we confess, He forgives (1 John 1:9). He throws our sins as far as the east is from the west (Psalm 103:12). And as Romans 8:1 reminds us, there is no condemnation for those who are in Christ Jesus.

So today, I'm grateful that while I can't rewrite my past, God is rewriting my present — and my eternity. That's worth more than one little letter.

Reflection Questions:

Is there a regret from your past that still shapes how you see yourself today?

How does remembering that you are an "ambassador for Christ" influence your daily choices?

What step could you take this week to represent Him well in your words or actions?

Prayer: Lord, thank You that my past doesn't define me — You do. Forgive me for the moments I've failed to represent You well, and help me to live today in a way that honors Your name. Teach me to see every word I speak and action I take as an opportunity to reflect Your character. Thank You for removing my condemnation and covering me with grace. Amen.

Day 7 – Untethered from the Lie That Depression Disqualifies You

Primary Scripture: "Bear one another's burdens, and thereby fulfill the law of Christ." – Galatians 6:2 (NASB95)

Supporting Scriptures: "We are destroying arguments and all arrogance raised against the knowledge of God, and we are taking every thought captive to the obedience of Christ." – 2 Corinthians 10:5 (NASB95)

"Finally, brothers and sisters, whatever is true, whatever is honorable, whatever is right, whatever is pure, whatever is lovely, whatever is commendable, if there is any excellence and if anything worthy of praise, think about these things." – Philippians 4:8 (NASB95)

"Therefore there is now no condemnation at all for those who are in Christ Jesus." – Romans 8:1 (NASB95)

Devotional:

Every day I open some platform of social media and see another post asking for prayer because someone has taken their own life. I've attended funerals for loved ones who have succumbed to the heaviness in their mind. It's heartbreaking. And here's the thing—Christians should be doing more to offer hope and help, not adding to the weight by treating depression like a taboo subject.

Too often, the evangelical community—especially those who haven't personally walked through depression—treats it like a character flaw or a lack of faith. But that's not the whole story. My husband, Shaun, loves me, loves the Lord, and has studied biblical counseling. He has never struggled with depression. I love the Lord too, have studied the same material, and yet, I sometimes battle anxiety and depression. He doesn't experience it the way I do, but he sees me, loves me, and tries to minister to me in it—whether I'm texting him about a gospel connection I found in my morning reading, or whether I'm crying in the kitchen because my job applications are going nowhere.

On paper, I can list countless blessings—three incredible kids who know and love Jesus, years of ministry experience, and a mile-high stack of God's faithfulness in my life. But depression doesn't check my resume before it walks through the door. Some days it sits down in the living room and makes itself at home, uninvited. And the worst part? Church—the place that should be the safest to be honest—can sometimes feel the least safe. Vulnerability gets mistaken for weakness. People assume if you're sad, you're either in sin, not reading your Bible enough, or simply not trusting God.

The truth? My struggle with depression isn't because I don't love God or because I'm hiding sin. In fact, if I didn't know His Word and His love, I might not be here at all. Like Paul, I understand what he meant when he wrote, "For to me, to live is Christ and to die is gain" (Phil. 1:21). Heaven will be perfect—but until then, I live here, in a fallen world, under Jesus' authority, for His purpose. That means I'll face suffering. You will too.

And I'm in good company. One of the greatest preachers of all time, Charles Spurgeon, wrestled with depression. His writings admit to seasons where sorrow showed up "without any real reason" but still gripped his mind. If depression disqualified you from serving God, we wouldn't have Spurgeon's sermons today. But they still inspire, teach, and counsel millions—even after his death.

So if you struggle, don't believe the lie that you're useless for the Kingdom. That's exactly the attack Satan wants you to believe—because if he can sideline you, he doesn't have to deal with you spreading the gospel. And if you don't struggle? Please, extend grace to those of us who do. Sometimes we just need someone to "hold space" for us—

to walk beside us without judgment, without trying to fix us, gently pointing us back to Jesus.

You don't have to have it all together to represent Him well. You don't have to feel strong to keep your hands on the plow. You don't have to be perfect to be effective. Broken crayons still color.

Reflection Questions:

How have you personally seen the church handle (or mishandle) conversations about depression?

What lies has the enemy tried to tell you about your worth or usefulness when you're struggling?

Who in your life needs you to "hold space" for them this week, and how can you practically show up for them?

Prayer: Lord, thank You that my worth and usefulness in Your Kingdom aren't dependent on my feelings or my mental health. Thank You for reminding me that depression does not disqualify me from serving You. Help me take every thought captive to the obedience of Christ and focus on what is true, pure, and lovely. Give me the courage to be vulnerable when I need help and the compassion to hold space for others who are struggling. May my life—especially in my weakness—reflect Your strength and Your glory. Amen.

Section 2 – Wrestling & Refining (Days 8–14)

Day 8 – Attitude and Leadership

Primary Scripture "Whatever you do, work at it with all your heart, as working for the Lord, not for human masters." — Colossians 3:23 (NIV)

Supporting Scriptures "For all have sinned and fall short of the glory of God." — Romans 3:23 (NIV)

"Follow my example, as I follow the example of Christ." — 1 Corinthians 11:1 (NIV)

Devotional:

Leadership is a topic we talk about a lot in our house. We even read about it together—one leadership book a month is pretty standard for us. Extreme Ownership by Jocko Willink and It's Your Ship by Michael Abrashoff are two of our favorites. But since not everyone has read them, I'll stick with a movie quote—

In Remember the Titans (a family favorite), there's a scene where one player says to the captain, "Attitude reflects leadership, Captain." That line stuck with me.

It also reminds me of something my high school band director did. He had us write down the alphabet, give each letter a number (A = 1, B = 2... Z = 26), then write out the word "attitude" and add up the numbers. The total? 100%.

Cue the dramatic reveal of our new band shirts that read: "Attitude is Everything!"

And it's true—your attitude is directly tied to your leadership. Whatever or whoever you're letting lead you will be reflected in your attitude. Yes, coaches, teachers, bosses, and mentors have their place. But beyond Friday night lights, game days, grades, paychecks, and retirement—who is really your leader?

If you're following Jesus, your attitude should reflect His. That means you're not the captain calling the shots—not you, your parents, your coach, your boss, or your college. You're working for the Lord. And when you follow His leadership, what you produce—in the classroom, the workplace, at home, or in your community—will be the best it can be.

Life changes. Coaches retire, bosses move on, and seasons shift. But Jesus' leadership never changes, and it never leads you astray. Since "attitude" adds up to 100%, you might as well make it 100% under His direction. Untether yourself from leadership that doesn't reflect Christ, and let your life be a reflection of His perfect example.

Reflection Questions

Who or what is currently shaping your attitude the most?

How does your attitude reflect (or not reflect) the leadership of Jesus in your life?

What's one practical step you can take today to align your leadership influences with Christ?

Prayer: Lord, thank You for being the perfect leader. Help me to recognize when my attitude is shaped by anything other than You. Teach me to follow Your example in humility, obedience, and love. Lead me to make choices that reflect Your heart and bring You glory. May my attitude be 100% Yours today. Amen.

Day 9 – Thankful for the Rain

Primary Scripture "Consider it pure joy, my brothers and sisters, whenever you face trials of many kinds, because you know that the testing of your faith produces perseverance."— James 1:2–3 (NIV)

Supporting Scriptures "Let us acknowledge the LORD; let us press on to acknowledge him. As surely as the sun rises, he will appear; he will come to us like the winter rains, like the spring rains that water the earth." — Hosea 6:3 (NIV)

"Give thanks in all circumstances; for this is God's will for you in Christ Jesus." — 1 Thessalonians 5:18 (NIV)

Devotional:

There have been many times I've prayed for rain over hayfields and crops, but one Texas summer stands out above the rest — over 100 days of 100+ degrees with no rain. I think even people who had never prayed before started talking to God! When rain finally came, we didn't just watch it from the porch; we ran out to dance in it, soaking up every drop like parched ground. You could almost hear the fields sigh with relief.

But where we live now, rain is a regular visitor. No prayers needed — sometimes we even find ourselves tempted to pray it away. Add to that the fact my titanium parts can now predict the weather, and my hip groans with every approaching storm. On those days, I'm far more thankful for the massage chair than the clouds overhead. Sunshine just makes me happy.

One day, as I sat talking with the Lord while rain poured from morning till night, I realized something: without the rain, I wouldn't truly appreciate the sun. Cold, gray days make the warmth and light of the sun feel like a gift I might otherwise take for granted. The same is true for the hard seasons of life — the trials, disappointments, and growing pains. They have a way of cultivating gratitude in our hearts for the deliverance, healing, and joy that follow.

James 1 tells us to "consider it joy" when we face trials, because they produce perseverance. No rain? No growth. No difficulty? No endurance. That perspective changes everything.

The next day, I sat outside like a lizard on a fence post, soaking up every golden ray. And before I thanked God for the sunshine, I thanked Him for the cold, rainy day before — because without it, I wouldn't have appreciated the light nearly as much.

Maybe we all need to pause and reflect on the "rainy days" in our lives — those uncomfortable, inconvenient, or even painful seasons — and recognize them as the backdrop that makes the "sunshine" shine brighter. When we untether ourselves from the discomfort and tether ourselves to the growth God produces through it, our gratitude deepens, and our faith strengthens.

Reflection Questions

What "rainy season" in your life has helped you appreciate the "sunshine" more?

How can you shift your perspective to see trials as opportunities for growth?

What specific blessing in your life today can you trace back to a difficult season?

Prayer: Lord, thank You for both the sunshine and the rain in my life. Help me to see trials not as interruptions, but as part of the growth You are producing in me. Teach me to find joy in the process, even when the skies are gray. May my gratitude deepen as I learn to trust You in every season. And when the sun does shine again, may I never forget to thank You first for the rain. Amen.

Day 10 – You Are Not Your Own

Primary Scripture "Or do you not know that your body is a temple of the Holy Spirit who is in you, whom you have from God, and that you are not your own? For you have been bought with a price: therefore, glorify God in your body." — 1 Corinthians 6:19–20 NASB95

Supporting Scripture(s) "Do nothing from selfishness or empty conceit, but with humility consider one another as more important than yourselves; do not merely look out for your own personal interests, but also for the interests of others. Have this attitude in yourselves which was also in Christ Jesus…" — Philippians 2:3–5 NASB95

"For to me, to live is Christ and to die is gain." — Philippians 1:21 NASB95

Devotional:

I've loved every stage of my kids' lives—babies, toddlers, preteens, and yes, even teenagers. (I know, some of you gasped just now.) Their teenage and young adult years have brought some of the best conversations, often sparked by their college courses.

One day, Gracie brought me her Theology assignment on moralistic therapeutic deism. Sounds fancy, right? In plain terms, it's the belief that life is about being a good person, feeling good about yourself, and seeing God as far-off—without repentance, obedience, or the reality of suffering. As we discussed, we both saw how much this mindset saturates today's culture: Do whatever makes you happy. Put yourself first. YOLO.

But here's the thing—it doesn't line up with God's Word. Philippians 2 tells us to "do nothing from selfishness" and to value others above ourselves. The Christian life is about humility, service, sacrifice, and obedience to Christ—not self-worship. When we live for ourselves, we quietly make ourselves the god we serve.

Self-care isn't wrong. Jesus Himself took time to rest. But self-care becomes dangerous when it's rooted in the belief that life is about me. Scripture reminds us: we were "bought with a price" (1 Corinthians 6:20). Our lives are not our own. We belong to Jesus, and that changes everything—from our priorities to our daily attitudes.

When you untether from worldly ideologies and tether yourself to God's truth, you're no longer chasing what's temporary. You're living for what's eternal.

Reflection Questions

In what ways has the "me first" mindset shown up in your own thinking or habits?

How would your daily priorities shift if you lived fully as someone "bought with a price"?

What worldly ideologies do you need to untether from in order to better follow Christ?

Prayer: Lord, thank You for the reminder that I am not my own. You purchased me at a great cost, and I belong to You. Help me to resist the temptation to put myself first and instead seek to serve others as You did. Show me where I've allowed worldly thinking to shape my actions, and give me the courage to untether from it. May my life reflect Your love, humility, and truth in every season. Amen.

Day 11 – Me Too

Primary Scripture "But He said to me, 'My grace is sufficient for you, for My power is made perfect in weakness.' Therefore I will boast all the more gladly about my weaknesses, so that Christ's power may rest on me."— 2 Corinthians 12:9 NIV

Supporting Scripture(s)"Carry each other's burdens, and in this way you will fulfill the law of Christ."— Galatians 6:2 NIV

"Though one may be overpowered, two can defend themselves. A cord of three strands is not quickly broken."— Ecclesiastes 4:12 NIV

Devotional:

Sometimes I am my own worst enemy. My brain runs laps around every "what if" and "what about" until I've worked myself into a full-on mental storm. I know Philippians 4:6 says, "Do not be anxious about anything…," and I'm working on it, y'all. But if you've ever battled anxiety or overthinking, you know this: you can understand the truth logically, yet still need to drag your feelings onto the train of obedience and force them to follow.

That's why " me too" moments matter so much.

Recently, I joined my husband on a work trip and spent time with several of the wives of his teammates. Every single one of them had been through the same season I'm in now. They understood. They listened. They shared. We laughed and nodded our way through conversation after conversation: "Gurl, me too!"

It happened again just the other day when I reached out to a friend God had put on my heart. We talked honestly about our struggles, encouraged each other, and walked away knowing we weren't alone. That's biblical. The enemy loves to isolate us because we're easier to pick off alone—just like predators go after animals that stray from the herd.

From MOPS groups to Bible studies to simple coffee dates, community gives us those "me too" moments that keep us tethered to truth and each other. Vulnerability is not weakness—it's courage. As Brene Brown says, it's where connection happens. Yes, use wisdom about who you open up to, but do open up. Jump in the trench with someone. Carry each other's burdens.

We are all broken crayons. And broken crayons still color—sometimes they create the most beautiful masterpieces because we let God's strength shine through our weakness.

Reflection Questions

Who in your life can you be vulnerable with about your struggles?

When was the last time you reached out and created a "me too" moment for someone else?

What fears or beliefs hold you back from letting others into your struggles?

Prayer: Lord, thank You for creating us for community. Thank You for the people in my life who remind me I am not alone. Help me to be brave enough to be vulnerable, to carry the burdens of others, and to allow them to help carry mine. Teach me to see my weaknesses as an opportunity for Your power to be displayed. Amen.

Day 12 – Hinds' Feet

Primary Scripture "The Sovereign LORD is my strength; He makes my feet like the feet of a deer, He enables me to tread on the heights."— Habakkuk 3:19 NIV

Supporting Scripture(s) "He makes my feet like the feet of a deer; He causes me to stand on the heights."— Psalm 18:33 NIV

"He makes my feet like the feet of a deer; He causes me to stand on the heights."— 2 Samuel 22:34 NIV

"And with your feet fitted with the readiness that comes from the gospel of peace."— Ephesians 6:15 NIV

Devotional:

If you've ever seen an Alpine ibex standing on a sheer cliff with a green valley far below, you might wonder—How did he get up there? Why would he even try? The truth is, God designed him for it. His hind feet can grip impossible terrain, keeping him surefooted where predators can't follow. He can climb to where the best food is found and find safety on high ground.

Scripture says God makes our feet like hinds' feet—capable of walking surefooted in seemingly impassable places. When we are pursuing the Lord, He enables us to climb higher spiritually, emotionally, and even through life's most treacherous seasons.

And here's the thing: in the same way "hinds' feet" shows up more than once in Scripture, so does another phrase—fear not. God's repetition is never by accident. Over and over (Joshua 1:9, Isaiah 43:1, Deuteronomy 31:6, Matthew 28:20) He reminds us that we don't have to be afraid because He is with us wherever we go.

If my spiritual feet are like hinds' feet, I can climb whatever path He sets before me—not because it's easy, but because He has equipped me for it. And when my feet are shod with the gospel of peace (Ephesians 6:15), I can stop at nothing in pursuing Christ and sharing His good news with others, even if the path feels steep.

The same God who created the ibex to walk impossible paths has designed you to navigate the terrain He's called you to. You don't have to fear the cliffs ahead—He's already equipped you to climb them, and He'll be with you every step of the way.

Reflection Questions

What "steep cliff" or challenge are you facing right now?

How has God already equipped you to handle it?

Where might fear be tethering you from stepping onto the path God has called you to?

Prayer: Lord, thank You for making my feet like hinds' feet, able to walk surefooted in the places You've called me to go. Help me trust Your design for my life, even when the path seems steep or uncertain. Remind me that You are with me and that fear has no place in the life of one who follows You. Give me boldness to keep climbing in pursuit of You and to share the gospel wherever You lead. Amen.

Day 13 – Belonging

Primary Scripture "Praise be to the God and Father of our Lord Jesus Christ, who has blessed us in the heavenly realms with every spiritual blessing in Christ. For He chose us in Him before the creation of the world to be holy and blameless in His sight. In love He predestined us for adoption to sonship through Jesus Christ, in accordance with His pleasure and will." — Ephesians 1:3–5 NIV

Supporting Scripture(s) "Before I formed you in the womb I knew you, before you were born I set you apart." — Jeremiah 1:5 NIV

"For You created my inmost being; You knit me together in my mother's womb." — Psalm 139:13 NIV

"They will see His face, and His name will be on their foreheads." — Revelation 22:4 NIV

Devotional:

Everybody wants to feel like they belong. The water tower in Prince George, Virginia even declares, "You Belong Here." But belonging has been something I've wrestled with my whole life.

As an Air Force brat, we moved constantly. I wasn't "from" anywhere, and I didn't have deep hometown roots or lifelong friends. My dad was adopted, and while I loved the grandparents who raised him, I always wondered about the family history I didn't know. For years, we believed we had Native American heritage on my dad's side. I embraced it, studied it, celebrated it... until a DNA test and a recovered piece of his adoption record revealed it wasn't true. It felt like someone had yanked the rug out from under my sense of identity.

Later, when we moved from my husband's hometown—the first place I'd truly felt at home—it hit me harder than expected. People would ask where I was from, and I'd stumble over the answer because... I didn't really have one. That's when God reminded me of the truth found in Ephesians 1.

I love to do an "Identity Check" exercise from the first two chapters of Ephesians, highlighting everything Scripture defines me as in Christ. Here's part of my list: blessed, chosen, loved, adopted, redeemed, forgiven, marked, and God's possession. That's powerful—especially when you feel unwanted, overlooked, or out of place.

Revelation 22:4 says His name will be on our foreheads. It makes me think of Toy Story—Buzz and Woody both belong to Andy because his name is written on their feet. If I ever got a tattoo, I'd be tempted to put "Jesus" on the bottom of mine, because I belong to Him.

I may not have an impressive earthly heritage, but my roots run deeper than this world. God knew me before I was even formed (Jeremiah 1:5), He knit me together with care (Psalm 139:13), and He adopted me into His family through Jesus Christ. My citizenship is in heaven, my belonging is in the body of Christ, and my identity is in being a daughter of the King. And if you're in Christ, this is true for you too!

So no matter where we live, no matter what our earthly story says, we can stand confident—we are wanted, chosen, loved, and secure. We belong as we tether ourselves tightly to Him.

Reflection Questions

Have you ever placed your sense of belonging in something temporary? How did that turn out?

What does your "Identity Check" list from Ephesians 1–2 look like right now?

How can remembering your eternal identity in Christ change the way you see your present circumstances?

Prayer: Father, thank You for choosing me before the creation of the world and adopting me into Your family through Jesus. When I feel out of place or disconnected, remind me of how you define me in Christ—blessed, chosen, loved, and secure. Help me live out of my heavenly identity and extend the same belonging to others who feel lost. Keep my eyes fixed on my true home with You. Amen.

Day 14 – Rescue Mission

Primary Scripture "The Spirit of the Lord is upon Me, because He has anointed Me to proclaim good news to the poor. He has sent Me to proclaim liberty to the captives and recovery of sight to the blind, to set at liberty those who are oppressed."— Luke 4:18 ESV

Supporting Scriptures "And I will put enmity between you and the woman, and between your offspring and hers; He will crush your head, and you will strike His heel."— Genesis 3:15 NIV

"Now is the time for judgment on this world; now the prince of this world will be driven out."— John 12:31 NIV

"When I saw Him, I fell at His feet as though dead. Then He placed His right hand on me and said: 'Do not be afraid. I am the First and the Last. I am the Living One; I was dead, and now look, I am alive for ever and ever! And I hold the keys of death and Hades.'"— Revelation 1:17–18 NIV

Devotional:

I love military and leadership books. They're filled with stories of courage, sacrifice, and strategy—traits we often connect to Navy SEALs, Green Berets, Rangers, Marines, and other elite warriors. These men and women are trained to run toward danger, to protect the vulnerable, and to give their lives for others if necessary.

I'll be honest—while I've always seen Jesus as the ultimate hero, I didn't often picture Him with those same warrior attributes. But Bible study has changed that.

In Nancy Guthrie's Blessed, she unpacks John's vision of Jesus in Revelation 1. This isn't the carpenter from Nazareth in sandals and a simple robe—this is the risen, reigning King. His robe and sash declare His role as both High Priest and King. His hair is white like wool, showing His wisdom and eternality. His eyes blaze like fire—penetrating, purifying, unstoppable. His feet are burnished bronze—tested, unshakable. His voice roars like many waters—powerful and commanding. From His mouth comes a double-edged sword—His Word, which brings grace to His people and judgment to His enemies. No wonder John fell at His feet as though dead.

Then in Ben Stuart's Rest and War, I saw another dimension—Jesus on the ultimate rescue mission. Stuart compares His coming to Earth to a HALO (High Altitude Low Opening) military jump. Jesus descended from the highest heaven, landing in the lowliest position—a baby in a manger. He came to liberate the captives, destroy the works of the enemy, and win a war we could never fight on our own.

From Genesis 3:15, the mission was clear—He would crush the serpent's head. In Luke 4:18, He declares His intent to set the oppressed free. In John 12:31, He announces the enemy's eviction notice. And in Revelation 1:18, He holds the keys to death and Hades in His hands.

Like a soldier throwing himself on a grenade to save his brothers, Jesus laid down His life on the cross—not for a squad or a platoon—but for the entire world.

Seeing Him as both Savior and Warrior grows my trust in Him. He is not only tender but also terrifying to His enemies. Not only compassionate, but also commanding. And He is always victorious.

That's why one pass through Scripture will never be enough. You don't train for war once and stop—you keep preparing, keep sharpening, keep knowing your Commander. As I study His Word, I have to untether from my own assumptions and let His truth form my understanding. And every time, I find my confidence in Him growing stronger.

Reflection Questions

How do you usually picture Jesus—gentle, powerful, or both? Why?

How does seeing Jesus as a warrior change the way you follow Him?

What "captivity" in your life do you need Him to set you free from today?

Prayer: Jesus, thank You for coming on the greatest rescue mission in history. Thank You for crushing the enemy, breaking the chains of sin, and securing victory over death. Help me to see You not just as my gentle Shepherd, but also as my fierce Warrior and King. Give me courage to follow wherever You lead, knowing You've already won the battle. Amen.

Section 3 – Anchoring to Truth (Days 15–22)

Day 15 – Where Does Your Theology Come From?

Primary Scripture "For the word of God is living and active and sharper than any two-edged sword ,and piercing as far as the division of soul and spirit, of both joints and marrow, and able to judge the thoughts and intentions of the heart."— Hebrews 4:12 NASB95

Supporting Scriptures "For whoever keeps the whole law and yet stumbles in one point, he has become guilty of all."— James 2:10 NASB95

"What is man that You remember him, or the son of man that You care for him? Yet You have made him a little lower than the angels, And You crown him with glory and majesty!"— Psalm 8:4–5 NASB95

Devotional:

It's funny how simple moments can turn into teachable ones. One day, I was mid-history lesson with our kids when our outside dogs went nuts at the fence line. The baying was relentless, so I went to investigate and found a nine-banded armadillo cornered and in need of rescue. History could wait—biology had just walked up the driveway!

That's the beauty of nontraditional teaching: you grab opportunities as they come, and sometimes the lesson sticks even better. The same thing happens in our family when watching movies—Christian or not. We've had some great theological conversations thanks to scenes that didn't quite line up with Scripture.

Case in point: not long ago, my daughter Gracie (with maximum sarcasm) said, "But I thought all sins are equal," while watching a character in front of a copy of the Lord's Prayer claim murder was the worst sin of all. She knew better—James 2:10 clearly says that stumbling in even one point makes us guilty of breaking the whole law. That knowledge didn't come from movies. It came from reading the Bible.

See, it's easy to choose the shortcut. In high school, I may or may not have used CliffsNotes on "Great Expectations" (no regrets). But when it comes to knowing God, His character, and His ways, secondhand summaries won't cut it. Devotionals, commentaries, books, and even movies can help us think about truth and they're great—but they are not the truth itself. God's Word is.

And here's the thing: you won't spot the false teaching or subtle distortion if you don't know the real thing. Hollywood's job is to entertain, not to make sure their script is 100% theologically sound. That's why we've fielded questions like, "Do we become angels when we die?" Spoiler: no. Angels and humans are both created beings. God made each "after its own kind" (Genesis). Psalm 8:5 tells us humans were created a little lower than angels, and 1 Corinthians 6 says we will one day judge them.

If you're not reading the Bible for yourself, you're relying on someone else's interpretation. That's dangerous. Even the best teachers and writers (myself included) are human and can get it wrong. God can't. His Word is always right, always relevant, and always the final authority.

So yes, enjoy your movies, studies, and devotionals—but don't neglect the source material. Always measure what you hear and see against Scripture, and let it correct you when needed. Untether yourself from the world's theology and tether yourself to the living, active, unchanging Word of God.

(And yes, if you didn't read the all-caps "READ YOUR BIBLE" in a southern accent with a head weave and a clap after each word... you missed out. Or didn't grow up in our house or youth group!)

Reflection Questions

How much of your understanding of God has come from the Bible itself versus secondhand sources?

When's the last time you spotted a false teaching because you knew what Scripture actually says?

What steps can you take to make sure God's Word—not entertainment or opinion—remains your ultimate authority?

Prayer: Lord, thank You for giving me Your Word as the unshakable foundation for truth. Help me to be faithful in reading and studying it for myself, not just relying on others to tell me what it says. Give me discernment to recognize and reject anything that contradicts Your truth. Anchor my heart in Scripture so I'm not swayed by opinion, culture, or convenience. Amen.

Day 16 – We Have the Cure

Primary Scripture

"If you declare with your mouth, 'Jesus is Lord,' and believe in your heart that God raised him from the dead, you will be saved." – Romans 10:9 (NIV)

Supporting Scriptures

"Always be prepared to give an answer to everyone who asks you to give the reason for the hope that you have. But do this with gentleness and respect." – 1 Peter 3:15 (NIV)

"You will be my witnesses in Jerusalem, and in all Judea and Samaria, and to the ends of the earth." – Acts 1:8 (NIV)

"Go and make disciples of all nations, baptizing them in the name of the Father and of the Son and of the Holy Spirit, and teaching them to obey everything I have commanded you." – Matthew 28:19–20 (NIV)

Devotional:

I'm back on movies again—who's seen The Maze Runner series? I read the books first (they were better, naturally), but it wasn't until the movies that I caught the allegorical element. Sometimes I'm slow, or maybe I just need a visual!

Thomas shows up in the Glade different from everyone else. He refuses to just blend in. He ends up being the one who helps them escape and—spoiler—his blood contains the cure for humanity. Now, The Maze Runner isn't a Christian movie, and Thomas isn't Jesus, but I couldn't miss the parallel. By the end, you're ready to run around vaccinating the whole world because you know the cure is real.

We have a cure too—but it's far greater than anything in fiction. And we don't even need a syringe. We have the gospel.

While studying Acts with our youth, I noticed how Paul adjusted his approach depending on the audience. In Acts 17:16–34, he speaks to the people of Athens in a way that resonates with them culturally and intellectually. In Acts 22:3, when speaking to Jews who knew his past, he shares his personal story.

Two of our professors once said:

"If you know enough to be saved, you know enough to lead someone to Christ." – Dr. Matt Queen

And another truth that stuck with me:

"No one can refute your personal story about what Christ has done in your life." – Dr. Seiberhagen

One of the most helpful things I've done is write down my testimony. Putting it into words forces you to reflect on what God has done. Your testimony is one of your most powerful tools for sharing the gospel—because it's your story of how Jesus changed you, backed by the truth of Scripture.

We once did this with our youth group, asking each student to write their testimony. One young man realized in the process that he wasn't actually saved. It wasn't that he was intentionally deceiving himself—he just never had that moment of realizing his sin and surrendering to Christ. God used a simple exercise, my own testimony, and Scripture to open his eyes.

That's why I like the FIRE approach:

Family – Ask about theirs, share about yours.

Interest – Talk hobbies, sports, or pets, and share your own.

Religion – Ask about holidays like Christmas or Easter, and share why you celebrate.

Evangelism – Transition naturally into your testimony or the gospel.

The point? Be intentional. Everyday conversations can lead to gospel opportunities if we're listening for them. And no—you don't need to have all the answers. When someone asks you a question you can't answer, it's okay to say, "I'm not sure, but let's find out together." That's discipleship—walking alongside someone in faith and learning together.

Jesus didn't just call us to make converts. He called us to make disciples—people who will grow in the Word and pass it on. So untether yourself from the fear that you don't know enough. You have the cure. And if you know enough to be saved, you know enough to lead someone else to Christ.

Reflection Questions

What is your personal testimony, and have you ever written it down to help you share it clearly?

Who can you practice using a tool like FIRE with to help you have a gospel conversation?

Who in your life might need to hear the cure of the gospel this week?

Prayer: Lord, thank You for the gift of salvation and the life-changing truth of the gospel. Help me to be bold yet gentle in sharing my faith with others. Give me opportunities to tell my story and connect it to Your story of redemption. Teach me to see everyday conversations as invitations to point people toward You. Use my words, my actions, and my life to make disciples for Your kingdom. Amen.

Day 17 – What's Your Ministry?

Primary Scripture 2 Corinthians 5:14–21 (NIV) 14 For Christ's love compels us, because we are convinced that one died for all, and therefore all died. 15 And he died for all, that those who live should no longer live for themselves but for him who died for them and was raised again. 16 So from now on we regard no one from a worldly point of view. Though we once regarded Christ in this way, we do so no longer. 17 Therefore, if anyone is in Christ, the new creation has come: The old has gone, the new is here! 18 All this is from God, who reconciled us to himself through Christ and gave us the ministry of reconciliation: 19 that God was reconciling the world to himself in Christ, not counting people's sins against them. And he has committed to us the message of reconciliation. 20 We are therefore Christ's ambassadors, as though God were making his appeal through us. We implore you on Christ's behalf: Be reconciled to God. 21 God made him who had no sin to be sin for us, so that in him we might become the righteousness of God.

Supporting Scripture Matthew 28:18–20 (NIV) 18 Then Jesus came to them and said, "All authority in heaven and on earth has been given to me. 19 Therefore go and make disciples of all nations, baptizing them in the name of the Father and of the Son and of the Holy Spirit,20 and teaching them to obey everything I have commanded you. And surely I am with you always, to the very end of the age."

Devotional:

Have you ever struggled with your place in church? Not the building — we know the building is just that, a facility where the actual church (the local body of believers) gathers. But have you ever felt like you wanted to DO something "in church," to serve in some way, but weren't sure how or if you could? Felt like you didn't want to just be a consumer who "goes to church" but doesn't live it out? That little nudge? That's the Holy Spirit.

Here's the thing: the church isn't Sunday mornings or Wednesday nights. It's us — the people — living out our faith at school, at work, in the store, in the stands at the ball game. Your ministry is not "someday when you have more time or training." You already have one.

Did you catch it in the verses above? You already have a ministry — and a title. God gave you the ministry of reconciliation and called you an ambassador for Christ. Your job is to live and speak in a way that draws people to be reconciled to God through Christ.

That doesn't mean you have to host a Bible study, teach Sunday school, or speak to crowds (you can, but that's not the only way). It's everyday life where people are reached. Like yesterday's reminder: "If you know enough to be saved, you know enough to lead someone to Christ."

You don't need a seminary degree. You've got the Bible, the Spirit, and a mission straight from Jesus Himself (Matthew 28). Care for the people in your life. Love them. Serve them. Share truth when the opportunity comes.

Untether yourself from the lie that you aren't "qualified" and just start. Your ministry is already in motion. Let's BE the church.

Reflection Questions

Where do you already see opportunities to "be the church" outside of Sunday gatherings?

What fears or excuses keep you from stepping into the ministry God has already given you?

How can you intentionally live out the role of "ambassador for Christ" this week?

Prayer: Lord, thank You for calling me into Your ministry, not because I'm qualified, but because You are. Help me see my role as an ambassador for Christ in every setting — at home, at work, and in my community. Give me courage to speak and act in ways that point people toward reconciliation with You. Remind me that my ministry starts right where I am. Amen.

Day 18 – Writing Your Story

Primary Scripture"...that if you confess with your mouth Jesus as Lord, and believe in your heart that God raised Him from the dead, you will be saved; for with the heart a person believes, resulting in righteousness, and with the mouth he confesses, resulting in salvation."— Romans 10:9–10 NASB95

Supporting Scriptures "For all have sinned and fallen short of the glory of God."— Romans 3:23 NASB95

"For the wages of sin is death, but the gift of God is eternal life through Christ Jesus our Lord."— Romans 6:23 NASB95

"Therefore, just as through one man sin entered into the world, and death through sin, and so death spread to all mankind, because all sinned—"— Romans 5:12 NASB95

"For by grace you have been saved through faith; and this is not of yourselves, it is the gift of God; not a result of works, so that no one may boast."— Ephesians 2:8–9 NASB95

Devotional:

I've mentioned before that if you know enough to be saved, you know enough to lead someone to Christ. One of the best ways to do that? Write down your story—your testimony—and learn how to share it. Once you've figured out how to articulate it, it's much easier to work it into conversations naturally. The "how" may change depending on the person or situation, but it's still your story of how you came to faith in Jesus.

For me, that "how" sometimes shows up in the most unexpected places—like a gun shop classroom. As the owner of a gun shop and firearms training center, I get in front of classes weekly. Some are believers, some are not. The gospel usually doesn't show up in range safety briefings. But since I've got a captive audience, I tell my story every time. Kind of like Paul in jail—he couldn't go anywhere, and neither can my students until I'm done talking!

I even tie my testimony into sight alignment. (Yes, really.) Just like your front sight(the most important site and also GOD in this analogy) needs to be aligned with your target and in the center of your life (the rear site), our lives need to be aligned with Jesus. While explaining that, I share the "Romans Road" verses and tell how I came to know Christ.

I grew up Catholic, went to St. Mary's Catholic school on a military base while my dad was in the Air Force. I knew the Bible stories, I knew God was real, I knew Jesus died on the cross. But I thought salvation worked like a scale— do enough good to outweigh the bad. I felt guilt for my sin but didn't know that grace through faith, not works, was even a thing. Nobody had pointed me to Ephesians 2:8-9.

Then, at 13, a friend invited me to a Newsboys concert. Josh McDowell spoke, and when he said "relationship with Christ," it stopped me in my tracks. You can't have a relationship with George Washington—he's dead. But Jesus? He's alive. That meant everything in the Bible wasn't just history—it was living. And I had to do something with it.

Romans 10:9-10 hit me: confess Jesus as Lord, believe in my heart that God raised Him from the dead, and be saved. That night I repented of my sin, trusted Jesus as my Savior, and surrendered to Him as Lord—meaning everything I did from then on needed to run through the filter of His Word. I followed in believer's baptism a week later.

Here's the thing—just like front sight alignment in shooting determines where the bullet goes, aligning your life with Christ determines where your life goes. He's done the work; He's the atoning sacrifice. Our part is to follow and keep Him at the center.

If you have a testimony, write it down. Practice it. Share it. If you don't, and you realize you need to repent and believe in Jesus, you can do that right where you are. It's not about magic words—it's about repentance and belief. Then, start reading your Bible, connect with a local church or online teaching, and grow. And then tell someone your story.

Reflection Questions

Have you ever written your personal testimony in detail? If not, what's stopping you?

Who in your life right now needs to hear what God has done for you?

How can you begin to naturally work your story into everyday conversations? You've already seen a tool to help you!

Prayer: Lord, thank You for giving me a story worth telling. Thank You for rescuing me from my sin, giving me new life, and calling me to share that with others. Help me be bold in telling my story, whether in church, at work, or in unexpected places like a gun range. Let my words point people to You and not to me. Give me wisdom to know when and how to speak, and the courage to actually do it. Amen.

Day 19 – I've Acted Like Saul

Primary Scripture "But Samuel replied: 'Does the LORD delight in burnt offerings and sacrifices as much as in obeying the LORD? To obey is better than sacrifice, and to heed is better than the fat of rams.'" – 1 Samuel 15:22 (NIV)

Supporting Scriptures "Do everything without grumbling or arguing." – Philippians 2:14 (NIV) "If it is possible, as far as it depends on you, live at peace with everyone." – Romans 12:18 (NIV)

"For I am confident of this very thing, that He who began a good work among you will complete it by the day of Christ Jesus." – Philippians 1:6 (NASB 1995)

Devotional:

Who in their right mind wants to admit they're like Saul? And I'm talking "OG" Old Testament Saul from 1 Samuel—the one Israel begged for so they could be like all the other nations, and who later tried to murder David.

I've never tried to murder anyone, but I've definitely seen my motives line up a little too close to Saul's. In 1 Samuel 13, Saul got impatient and sacrificed instead of waiting for Samuel like he was supposed to. Why? Because he cared more about what the people thought than about obeying

God's timing. I've been there—making rash decisions to look good, or keeping my mouth shut when I should've spoken up for truth because I didn't want to make waves.

My daughter, watching a movie recently, said, "No response is a response, girl." Sometimes silence is wise—when we're angry and our words wouldn't be loving. But sometimes silence is condoning. I'm not talking about Facebook sparring matches; I'm talking about those moments when God's truth needs to be spoken in love, but we choose comfort instead.

Even "good" actions can be wrong if our hearts are in the wrong place. Saul's sacrifice was to the Lord, but it was about pleasing people. God prefers obedience over sacrifice (1 Sam 15:22). I've been guilty of people-pleasing too—scrolling back to see how my "biblical" posts were received. Ouch.

And let's be honest—avoiding confrontation with the silent treatment? Tempting. But God doesn't give the silent treatment. From Genesis to the Gospels, He speaks. Our words matter, and sometimes love means having the hard conversation.

A friend once taught me to pause and ask:

Does it need to be said?

Does it need to be said by me?

Does it need to be said right now?

I don't always get it right, but Philippians 1:6 reminds me He's not done with me yet. Let's untether from seeking approval from people and care most about the approval of the One who began the good work in us.

Reflection Questions

Can you think of a time when you acted out of people-pleasing instead of obedience to God? What happened?

How can you better discern when to speak and when to remain silent?

What would change in your daily decisions if you sought God's approval above all else?

Prayer: Lord, I confess that sometimes I care more about what people think than about what You think. Forgive me for the times I've chosen comfort over obedience. Help me to speak truth in love, to know when to speak and when to pause, and to keep my heart focused on You alone. Thank You that You're not done with me yet, and that You will complete the work You've started. Keep me tethered to Your will and untethered from the pull of people-pleasing. In Jesus' name, Amen.

Day 20 – Better Together

Primary Scripture: "Do nothing from selfish ambition or conceit, but in humility count others more significant than yourselves." – Philippians 2:3 (ESV)

Supporting Scripture: "From Him the whole body, joined and held together by every supporting ligament, grows and builds itself up in love, as each part does its work." – Ephesians 4:16 (NIV)

Devotional:

When I was in junior high and early high school, I hated group work. Not because I was antisocial (though I do enjoy some alone time) but because I didn't want my grade depending on someone else's work. Usually, I'd just take over, do it all myself, and hand it in so we'd get an A. Looking back, I'm not sure if that was because I thought I was smarter… or because I had trust issues. Probably both.

By my last couple years of high school, my perspective changed. I landed in a group with Prem, Alan, and Amanda—three of the sharpest and most creative people in our class. They each brought something I couldn't. We ended up producing work better than anything I could have done alone. That was my first taste of how much stronger we are when we pull together.

Fast forward to adulthood, and I've seen the same principle in the church. Everyone has something to contribute—whether they've been walking with Jesus for decades or just met Him yesterday. Sadly, I've also seen group "discussions" turn into theological sparring matches, especially around topics like Bible translations or denominational practices. Those debates may be fine in the right setting, but in front of new believers or non-believers, they can do more harm than good.

I've been guilty of it myself—getting so focused on being right that I lost sight of what's most important. The Holy Spirit has had to remind me: the goal is not to prove intelligence, it's to point people to Jesus. We're not called to compete for who can sound the most educated; we're called to work together to make disciples.

If you're usually the most knowledgeable person in the room—great. Use it to build up, not to boast. And if you feel like you have nothing to offer, remember: if you know enough to be saved, you know enough to share the gospel. We learn best when we learn together.

Reflection Questions:

Have you ever let pride or competition get in the way of encouraging someone's faith?

How can you better recognize and appreciate the unique gifts others bring to the "team"?

Is there a setting where you need to shift your focus from secondary issues to the gospel itself?

Prayer: Lord, thank You for the people You've placed in my life to teach, encourage, and sharpen me. Forgive me for the times I've let pride, comparison, or the need to be "right" get in the way of loving others well. Help me to focus on what matters most — You and Your gospel. Teach me to value the gifts of others, to bring my best, and to work together for Your glory. Amen.

Day 21 – Bring Our Best

Primary Scripture "Now there are varieties of gifts, but the same Spirit. And there are varieties of ministries, and the same Lord. There are varieties of effects, but the same God who works all things in all persons. But to each one is given the manifestation of the Spirit for the common good."— 1 Corinthians 12:4–7 NASB

Supporting Scripture(s)"How then are they to call on Him in whom they have not believed? How are they to believe in Him whom they have not heard? And how are they to hear without a preacher? But how are they to preach unless they are sent? Just as it is written: 'How beautiful are the feet of those who bring good news of good things!'"— Romans 10:14–15 NASB

"Go, therefore, and make disciples of all the nations, baptizing them in the name of the Father and the Son and the Holy Spirit, teaching them to follow all that I commanded you; and behold, I am with you always, to the end of the age."— Matthew 28:19–20 NASB

Devotional:

One time, my son Wesley and his sister were arguing about teamwork. Gracie threw out the classic line,

"There's no 'I' in team," and Wes, quick as ever, shot back with, "Well, in the words of my man Kobe, there is an M-E!"

Now, there actually is a "me" in team—but those two letters don't make the whole team, and neither do you. Still, your part matters. God designed you to bring your best to the table. Paul explained it in 1 Corinthians 12—every believer has spiritual gifts given by the Holy Spirit for the good of the Body of Christ.

It's not about being the most talented, the loudest, or the most "qualified." It's about showing up with what you have and giving it wholeheartedly for the sake of the gospel. And yes, teamwork in the Kingdom is older than any sports league.

One of my favorite illustrations comes from Dustin Willis in Life in Community. He compares the Body of Christ to a good old-fashioned church potluck. Everyone brings their specialty—Mrs. Polly's mac and cheese, Mr. Thompson's homemade vanilla bean ice cream, Mrs. White's unbeatable fried okra. Nobody tries to outdo each other. They just bring the dish they're best at making. The result? A table full of abundance where no one leaves hungry.

That's the Body of Christ. Your "dish" might be teaching, encouraging, serving, organizing, creating, or listening. It might be something quirky—like my son Tristan's card tricks—that God uses to open doors for gospel conversations. Whatever it is, bring it. Don't compare, don't hold back, and don't think it doesn't matter. Untether yourself from the lie that you don't have something to contribute and bring your best!

When each of us brings our best, we show the world a fuller picture of Jesus. That's not just good teamwork—that's Kingdom work.

Reflection Questions

What is one gift, talent, or skill God has given you that you can intentionally bring to serve others this week?

Have you been tempted to compare your "dish" to someone else's? How can you shift your focus back to faithfulness over comparison?

Where in your life—work, home, school, community—can you be intentional about bringing your best for the sake of the gospel?

Prayer: Lord, thank You for the unique gifts You have given me through Your Spirit. Forgive me for the times I've compared myself to others or held back what You've entrusted to me. Teach me to see the value of my contribution, no matter how small it feels. Help me to bring my best, not for my glory, but for Yours, and to trust that You will use it to build Your Kingdom. Show me opportunities this week to serve others with what I have, and give me the courage to step into them with joy. Amen.

Day 22 – Anchoring to Your Leader

Primary Scripture "Trust in the Lord with all your heart and do not lean on your own understanding. In all your ways acknowledge Him, and He will make your paths straight."— Proverbs 3:5–6

Supporting Scripture(s)

"Every way of a man is right in his own eyes, but the Lord weighs the heart." — Proverbs 21:2

"The heart is more deceitful than all else and is desperately sick; who can understand it?" — Jeremiah 17:9

"But God demonstrates His own love toward us, in that while we were yet sinners, Christ died for us." — Romans 5:8

"All this is from God, who reconciled us to Himself through Christ and gave us the ministry of reconciliation." — 2 Corinthians 5:18

Devotional:

You know that time of year when graduation announcements flood our mailboxes and social media feeds. For our family, we've had a couple of years that have been especially meaningful— like when our daughter Grace graduated and began her first official year as a full-time college sophomore. As former Directors of Students at First Baptist Grapeland, Shaun and I also walked alongside our oldest son's class from eighth grade to graduation. Thirteen students we'd known for years stepped into a brand-new season—exciting for some, intimidating for others.

For moments like these, Shaun and I have an "anchor verse" we often write in cards to graduates: Proverbs 3:5–6. But this truth isn't just for graduates—it's for all of us, in every season.

Scripture interprets Scripture, and we see that our "own understanding" is not to be trusted. Proverbs 21:2 says every man's way seems right to him, but the Lord weighs the heart. Jeremiah 17:9 reminds us that the heart is deceitful and sick. On our own, we simply can't chart the best course.

But God—how grateful I am for those two words! He loved us while we were still sinners (Romans 5:8), reconciled us through Christ (2 Corinthians 5:18), and now leads us. Trusting Him with all our hearts doesn't mean the road will be smooth. There will be storms, potholes, rocky cliffs—but He equips us, like the "hinds' feet" we discussed earlier, to handle the path He sets us on. And He promises His presence wherever we go.

So, whether you're stepping into a new job, new school year, or new chapter of life, anchor yourself to your Leader. Untether from your way. Trust Him fully. Follow His lead.

Reflection Questions

In what areas of your life are you tempted to "lean on your own understanding"?

How have you seen God guide you through difficult or unfamiliar terrain in the past?

What practical steps can you take to acknowledge Him in all your ways this week?

Prayer: Lord, thank You for being my Leader, my Guide, and my Anchor. Forgive me when I try to navigate life on my own and rely on my limited understanding. Help me to trust You with all my heart and to acknowledge You in everything I do. Direct my path in a way that brings You glory, and give me the courage to follow wherever You lead. Amen.

Section 4 – Walking in Hope (Days 23–30)

Day 23 – Sight Unseen

Primary Scripture "For we walk by faith, not by sight." – 2 Corinthians 5:7 (NASB)

Supporting Scriptures "Jesus said to him, 'Because you have seen Me, have you believed? Blessed are they who did not see, and yet believed.'" – John 20:29 (NASB)

"Trust in the LORD with all your heart and do not lean on your own understanding. In all your ways acknowledge Him, and He will make your paths straight." – Proverbs 3:5–6 (NASB)

Devotional:

Have you ever tried to walk in the dark behind someone who had a flashlight—but you didn't?

I learned quickly what that felt like one night in Texas while hog hunting. Shaun and his dad were ahead of me, racing toward the bay dogs with their catch dogs in tow. I was new at this and far less brave back then, so I hung back a little. It was pitch black, hogs were darting out around me, and I didn't have a flashlight. My heart was pounding, but I knew I had to keep moving forward and do my part. With no light of my own, I kept following their lead and whispering Philippians 4:13 under my breath—

way out of context, but clinging to the truth that my strength came from God.

Looking back now, I realize that's a lot like walking by faith. When Paul wrote that we "walk by faith, not by sight," he was talking about trusting in the truth of the gospel even when we haven't seen it for ourselves—something Jesus Himself affirmed in John 20:29. I find it easier to trust what I can see with my own eyes, but that's not really faith. Faith is trusting God's heart and His Word when you can't see the whole picture.

In this recent season of my life, God didn't hand me a detailed map. Instead, He gave me just enough light for the next step. And in hindsight, if I had seen the whole journey from the start, I might have missed the growth, the humility, and the awe that came from watching His faithfulness unfold. Walking by faith means I keep going—even when my feelings lag behind—trusting that in time the picture will become clearer, and I'll see His goodness in ways I never could have imagined.

Reflection Questions

When has God asked you to take a step of obedience before showing you the full plan?

What truths about God's character help you trust Him when you can't see the outcome?

Are there areas in your life where you're still trying to "walk by sight" instead of faith?

Prayer: Lord, thank You for being my light, even when I can't see the whole path ahead. Help me to trust Your character more than my circumstances. Teach me to walk in obedience, dragging my feelings along if I must, knowing that You will bring clarity in Your time. Strengthen my faith so that I lean on You instead of my own understanding, and let my life be a testimony of Your goodness and faithfulness. Amen.

Day 24 – Broken Crayons Still Color

Primary Scripture "But He said to me, 'My grace is sufficient for you, for power is perfected in weakness.' Most gladly, therefore, I will rather boast about my weaknesses, so that the power of Christ may dwell in me." – 2 Corinthians 12:9 (NASB)

Supporting Scriptures "For all have sinned and fall short of the glory of God." – Romans 3:23 (NASB)

"Therefore if anyone is in Christ, this person is a new creation; the old things passed away; behold, new things have come." – 2 Corinthians 5:17 (NASB)

"For I am confident of this very thing, that He who began a good work among you will complete it by the day of Christ Jesus." – Philippians 1:6 (NASB)

Devotional:

I'm not the inventor of the phrase broken crayons still color, but it's one that has stuck with me for years. I've seen it play out over and over in the lives of others—watching people cling to God through their brokenness and create something beautiful that becomes a survival guide for someone else going through the same thing. Seeing it in myself, however, has been another story.

Not long ago, I reminded a friend of this truth, only to find myself two weeks later declaring to my husband that I was useless because I was "too broken." Bless him—he puts up with a lot. He's like a hyper-saint in that way.

My boys, on the other hand, have grasped this lesson since they were young. When our youngest, Tristan, was about five, one of our dogs chewed the leg off his beloved warthog toy. I was headed to throw it away, but Tristan stopped me in tears, asking, "If I was wounded, would you just throw me out?" We still have that warthog—complete with medical tape on its leg.

Then there's our family's Christmas tree mascot: a glass dinosaur with a missing tail. Rather than toss him, I "healed" him with a bandage, and he still shines on the tree each year.

That's what our relationship with God is like. We are all broken by sin and the suffering of this world (Romans 3:23), but in Christ we are made new (2 Corinthians 5:17). The work He begins in us, He will finish (Philippians 1:6). And even in our weakness, His power is at work (2 Corinthians 12:9).

Being tethered to Jesus means that regardless of our brokenness—physical or emotional—we're still useful to the Creator. We are the warthog with the bandaged leg and the dino with the patched-up tail. Broken crayons still color, and in the hands of God, our brokenness can be a masterpiece.

Reflection Questions

What "broken" part of your life has God used to encourage someone else?

How does remembering God's power in your weakness change the way you see yourself?

Who in your life might need the reminder that broken crayons still color?

Prayer: Lord, thank You for not discarding me when I feel damaged or useless. Thank You for making beauty from my brokenness and for using my story to point others to You. Help me to trust that You are still at work in me, healing, restoring, and shaping me into who You've called me to be. Teach me to see my weakness as an opportunity for Your strength to shine. Amen.

Day 25 – Forever Forward

Primary Scripture "Not that I have already obtained it or have already become perfect, but I press on so that I may lay hold of that for which also I was laid hold of by Christ Jesus. Brothers and sisters, I do not regard myself as having laid hold of it yet; but one thing I do: forgetting what lies behind and reaching forward to what lies ahead, I press on toward the goal for the prize of the upward call of God in Christ Jesus." – Philippians 3:12–14 (NASB)

Supporting Scriptures "But prove yourselves doers of the word, and not just hearers who deceive themselves." – James 1:22 (NASB) "When I am afraid, I will put my trust in You." – Psalm 56:3 (NASB)

"For God has not given us a spirit of timidity, but of power and love and discipline." – 2 Timothy 1:7 (NASB)

Devotional:

I think I've found a new motto: Forever Forward. I've learned so much from God's creation—how to handle things, and sometimes how not to handle them. A nautilus, for example, never retreats to a smaller chamber once it grows. Each step forward is sealed off behind it. No matter what, it moves ahead.

Yet I've found myself, more times than I'd like to admit, paralyzed by what I think others might say or think. My son pointed out recently that I don't do that with matters of faith—because I fear God more than man—but in other areas, I sometimes let hypothetical opinions stop me cold.

History gives us another picture: in 1519, Hernán Cortés ordered his men to burn their ships upon reaching new land, leaving no way to retreat. Move forward or die trying. Spiritually speaking, many of us need to burn the ships in our own minds—the comfort zones, the excuses, the old identities others keep us trapped in—and choose growth.

Growth isn't always comfortable. Like the growing pains I had as a kid, it can ache, but it's a sign of movement. It's why James says to be doers of the Word, not just hearers. Doing means risk. Doing means movement. And doing means letting go of the old chambers behind you to embrace the unknown ahead.

Whatever it is that's tethering you—real opposition or imagined—seal off the past. Step forward in obedience to God's call. Forever forward.

Reflection Questions

What "old chambers" from your past do you still retreat to instead of moving forward?

Where might fear of others' opinions be holding you back from obeying God?

What is one practical step you can take today to "burn the ships" and move forward in faith?

Prayer: Lord, I confess that I have let fear—of failure, of change, of others' opinions—keep me from moving forward in obedience to You. Give me the courage to burn the ships, seal off the past, and trust You for each step ahead. Teach me to press on toward the prize, to grow through the pain, and to live with a forever forward mindset. Thank You for going before me and for walking beside me every step of the way. Amen.

Day 26 – Silencing the Voices

Primary Scripture "He says, 'Be still, and know that I am God; I will be exalted among the nations, I will be exalted in the earth.'" – Psalm 46:10 (NIV)

Supporting Scriptures "You keep him in perfect peace whose mind is stayed on You, because he trusts in You." – Isaiah 26:3 (ESV) "Come to Me, all you who are weary and burdened, and I will give you rest." – Matthew 11:28 (NIV) "Casting all your anxieties on Him, because He cares for you." – 1 Peter 5:7 (ESV)

Devotional:

Sometimes the loudest voices we need to quiet are the ones inside our own heads—the critics, the doubts, the endless noise that drowns out creativity and courage. I'm an overthinker, a worrier, and deeply empathetic. My mind runs 24/7 and even wakes me up in the middle of the night.

Over the years, writing blogs has been my anchor—journaling my thoughts and tying them to the truth of God's Word. But recently, I stumbled upon an unexpected tool for silencing the noise: painting.

I am not a painter. My mother, a former art teacher, can bring anything to life with a pencil or paintbrush. I, on the other hand, have always felt creatively clumsy with visual art—like a stick-figure prodigy at best. But on a whim, I walked into an art studio offering step-by-step painting classes. What I didn't expect was how much the process would demand my full attention. Mixing colors, following instructions, moving the brush—there was no room left for anxious thoughts.

The blank canvas was intimidating, but with each brushstroke I realized courage often looks like just starting. Painting has become a small but meaningful way to push past fear in a safe, creative space. It's also taught me something I've learned while hiking or standing on the rim of the Grand Canyon: when we're fully present in the moment, the noise fades, the earthly tether snaps, and God's voice comes into focus.

Sometimes silencing the voices means intentionally doing something that demands all of you—leaving your worries, social media, and to-do lists behind. And in that stillness, you might just find the peace God's been offering you all along.

Reflection Questions

What are the "voices" in your head that most often drown out God's truth?

When was the last time you were fully present in the moment? What were you doing?

What activity could you try this week to help you quiet your mind and focus on God?

Prayer: Lord, I confess that I often let the noise in my mind drown out Your still, small voice. Help me to be still and know that You are God. Show me healthy, life-giving ways to quiet the noise and turn my focus back to You. Thank You for being my peace, my refuge, and my anchor no matter what's swirling around me. Amen.

Day 27 – Know Your Enemy

Primary Scripture "For our struggle is not against flesh and blood, but against the rulers, against the powers, against the world forces of this darkness, against the spiritual forces of wickedness in the heavenly places." – Ephesians 6:12 (NASB)

Supporting Scriptures "The thief comes only to steal and kill and destroy; I came so that they would have life, and have it abundantly." – John 10:10 (NASB)

"Greater love has no one than this, that a person will lay down his life for his friends." – John 15:13 (NASB) "Now the salvation, and the power, and the kingdom of our God, and the authority of His Christ have come, for the accuser of our brothers and sisters has been thrown down, the one who accuses them before our God day and night." – Revelation 12:10 (NASB)

Devotional:

I hate realizing I've gotten out of the habit of regular study—and then seeing that I'm spiraling because of it. That's where I've been lately. My thought patterns haven't been in alignment with God's Word. And here's how I know: anytime I start viewing a person—or group of people—as the enemy, no matter what they've done, I've taken a wrong turn.

Because the enemy isn't flesh and blood.

Satan's playbook is well-documented in Scripture. He's not creative, but he's persistent—stealing joy, killing hope, destroying relationships, and sowing division. His ultimate goal is to erode our trust in God. And just like any wise military leader, we need to study our enemy's strategy: his patterns, his motivations, his past tactics.

But here's the good news—he doesn't win the war. Revelation 12:10 assures us that his defeat is certain. Until then, our job is to stand firm, put on the full armor of God (Ephesians 6:10–20), and refuse to give him ground in our hearts and minds.

In the Summer of 25, my family and I went to the Summer Worship Nights concert with Phil Wickham, Brandon Lake, and Josiah Queen. When Phil sang "Battle Belongs"—my anthem for the last six months—I stood with my hands lifted and tears streaming. In that moment, I was reminded that I've never fought alone. Worship is warfare.

When we kneel in surrender, heaven stands in victory. The battle truly belongs to the Lord.

Reflection Questions

Have you ever misidentified "the enemy" in your life? How did that impact your relationships?

Which of the enemy's tactics do you recognize most often in your own life?

How can you make worship a regular part of your spiritual warfare?

Prayer: Lord, thank You for clearly identifying the true enemy in Your Word. Forgive me when I aim my frustration and hurt at people instead of recognizing the spiritual battle at work. Help me to stand firm in Your armor, grounded in truth, and strengthened by Your Spirit. Remind me that the battle belongs to You and that in Christ, the victory is already won. Amen.

Day 28 – Dollar Store Heart, Designer Love

Primary Scripture "But God demonstrates His own love toward us, in that while we were still sinners, Christ died for us." – Romans 5:8 (NASB)

Supporting Scriptures "So God created man in His own image; in the image of God He created him; male and female He created them." – Genesis 1:27 (NKJV)

"See how great a love the Father has given us, that we would be called children of God; and in fact we are. For this reason the world does not know us: because it did not know Him." – 1 John 3:1 (NASB)

"I praise You, for I am fearfully and wonderfully made. Wonderful are Your works; my soul knows it very well." – Psalm 139:14 (ESV)

Devotional:

I told my husband today that I feel like a Dollar Store product—useful, sometimes even necessary, but never premium. Not the thing people show off. Not the thing they brag about. Just… there. Replaceable.

And the worst part? Even if I changed my appearance to look like someone who has it all together, inside I'd still feel like the knockoff version. The "close enough" that never quite measures up.

It's not about jealousy—it's about worth. And it's a battle I fight often.

Maybe you've been there, too. Maybe your struggle comes from imposter syndrome, childhood wounds, financial instability, or simply never feeling like you fit the mold. My version of femininity has never been frills and pearls. I'm rugged, hands-on, and practical. I've learned to "make it work" with what I have, and sometimes that mindset lingers long after the need for it is gone.

But here's the truth: my worth was never tied to my income, my appearance, or my ability to fit into someone else's definition of "enough." It was set by the One who created me in His image.

God didn't assign value based on bank accounts, social circles, or wardrobes. He didn't make some people "gold" and others "discount bin." Every single one of us bears His image, and in His eyes, that's priceless.

Even if we show up in camo and work boots instead of stilettos and a silk scarf, we are loved. We are chosen. We are worth the life of His Son. That's not Dollar Store—

that's divine. Untether yourself from the lies of the enemy and tether to the truth of God's Word!

Reflection Questions

What situations or lies tend to trigger feelings of "less-than" in your life?

How does knowing you are made in God's image shift your perspective on your worth?

What would change in your daily life if you fully believed God's view of you over your own feelings?

Prayer: Father, thank You for creating me in Your image and assigning my worth before I took my first breath. Forgive me for the times I've believed the lie that I'm not enough. Help me to see myself the way You see me—valuable, chosen, and loved. Let my life reflect the truth that in Christ, I am more than enough. Amen.

Day 29 – How Can I Ask for More?

Primary Scripture "He who did not spare His own Son, but delivered Him over for us all, how will He not also with Him freely give us all things?" – Romans 8:32 (NASB)

Supporting Scriptures "Let us then approach God's throne of grace with confidence, so that we may receive mercy and find grace to help us in time of need." – Hebrews 4:16 (NIV)

"For your Father knows what you need before you ask Him." – Matthew 6:8b (ESV)

"And if we know that He hears us in whatever we ask, we know that we have the requests which we have asked from Him." – 1 John 5:15 (NASB)

Devotional:

Since I've been so transparent about how I often feel about myself, I might as well share another confession: sometimes I struggle to ask God for more.

This isn't because I doubt His goodness—quite the opposite. I know He is good, all the time. I know His ways are higher, His plans perfect, His love unfailing. But when I think about what He's already done—when I think about the cross—it's hard for me to imagine asking for anything else.

As a mom of two sons, I can't fathom giving either of them up. Yet God gave His Son. And Jesus came willingly, knowing it would mean suffering and death for sins He didn't commit—mine included. That's the weight of what I mean when I say we are "worth dying for." It's not a feel-good slogan. It's the reality of a love so deep it acted in the most sacrificial way possible.

So how could I possibly ask for more?

Scripture tells me to come to Him, to pour out my heart, to pray without ceasing. I know He hears me, even when all I have is a sigh or a tear. Yet there's a quiet hesitation inside me—not because God is unapproachable, but because I feel like salvation alone should be more than enough.

Maybe you've felt it too—that pull between gratitude and need. But here's the truth: the same God who gave His Son also says we can come boldly to His throne. Not because we're entitled, but because His goodness and love invite us there.

He's not weary of your voice. He's not rolling His eyes at your prayers. He welcomes you—fully, always.

Reflection Questions

What holds you back from asking God for more when you need something?

How does Romans 8:32 reshape your understanding of God's willingness to bless you?

What is one prayer you've hesitated to pray that you could bring to Him today?

Prayer: Father, thank You for giving what was most precious—Your Son—to save me. Forgive me for the moments I let hesitation keep me from coming to You. Help me to remember that You invite me into Your presence, not because I deserve it, but because You are that good. Teach me to pray with both gratitude for what You've done and faith for what You can still do. Amen.

Day 30 – Lasers and Bible Study

Scripture: "All Scripture is breathed out by God and profitable for teaching, for reproof, for correction, and for training in righteousness, that the man of God may be complete, equipped for every good work."— 2 Timothy 3:16–17 (ESV)

Devotional:

As a firearms instructor and shooting sports enthusiast, I was thrilled to incorporate a laser into my shooting. Laser focus sounds like a great thing, right?

It is—but I quickly discovered something important: a laser is a great addition, but it can't replace the fundamentals. It doesn't make up for a poor grip, bad stance, or sloppy trigger control. It doesn't replace the knowledge of my iron sights, the ability to load a magazine, or the habit of chambering a round properly.

You can't throw the fundamentals out the window, aim where the laser points, and expect precision. True accuracy comes from integrating all the fundamentals—together, consistently.

It's the same with studying the Bible.

We can't simply rely on books about the Bible, devotionals on a particular topic, or a scattering of inspirational verses pulled out of context and expect to know the whole picture of who God is.

Those tools—just like a laser, just like this book—can be incredibly helpful and point you in the right direction. But they're not meant to replace the real thing: reading and studying God's Word in its entirety, in context, and with an understanding of its different genres and purposes.

The Bible contains history, poetry, prophecy, wisdom literature, and law. Within those, you'll find idioms, metaphors, analogies, irony, personification, hyperbole, and more. Cultural context matters—just like not everyone understands the phrase "it's raining cats and dogs," not everyone instantly understands a first-century Jewish idiom without study.

Studying Scripture is like mining for precious gems—you dig deeper, uncovering layers you never noticed before. But more than anything, remember this: the Bible is about God. He is always the main character. Untether from anything that isn't in alignment with what His Word says.

So when you read, ask: What is this teaching me about God? Because the more we know Him, the more we can love Him. And you can't truly love what you don't truly know.

Reflection Questions:

What "fundamentals" of Bible study do you tend to skip over or rush through?

Have you been solely relying on "tools" (like devotionals or commentaries) instead of spending time in the Word itself?

How can you deepen your understanding of the historical and cultural context of Scripture this week?

Prayer: Lord, thank You for giving us Your Word—living, active, and life-giving. Help me to handle it with care, to study it in context, and to seek You as the main character in every passage. Keep me grounded in the fundamentals, so that everything I learn builds on the truth You've revealed. Amen.

If you have made it this far, thank you, it is my hope that this book has pointed continually to Christ! If you're already a believer, the following will serve as me "putting my money where my mouth is," so to speak, as I encouraged everyone to write down their salvific testimony—a fancy way of saying the story about when you were saved. If you aren't a believer, and you're questioning and wondering, please keep reading. Maybe you're like me and know *about* Jesus but want to put all those pieces together. It is my hope and prayer that the sharing of my salvation testimony will help you in some way to decide to surrender fully to Jesus as I have.

My Salvation Testimony

I was raised Catholic and went to St. Mary's private Catholic school while living on a military base, as my dad was in the Air Force. Later he retired, and we moved to Texas. I understood the Bible as a historical textbook. I knew there were accounts of the life of Jesus outside of the Bible by groups of people who were not Christian that affirmed the historical existence of Jesus. I knew who God was and that Jesus had died on the cross, as well as the stories of the Bible. After Confirmation classes, I knew that I was a sinner—Romans 3:23 said that all have sinned and fallen short of the glory of God. I knew that sin was wrong and that it had to do with not being obedient to God, and I could recite the Apostles' Creed and the Ten Commandments. I knew *about* God.

When I was 13, one of my mother's coworker's sons invited me to a Newsboys concert. (We didn't listen to that kind of music in Mass!) I went, and Josh McDowell took the stage and called a verse of Scripture which I knew. I've always been fairly studious—and unfortunately prideful about it—and remember having a prideful attitude at that moment about knowing what he was about to say, until he expanded upon Romans in a way I never understood before. He then started to talk about relationships. A relationship with Christ struck me as an odd thing to say.

It occurred to me that I couldn't have a relationship with George Washington because he was dead, but Jesus was different. I'd heard those words, *resurrected on the third day,* more times than I can count. I heard Jesus was the Word who became flesh and dwelt among us from the book of John. I guess I didn't really think about *resurrection* meaning being dead and then raised to life—

being alive. I could have a relationship with someone who is alive.

I began all at once to see that the Bible was living and active right now, not a history text. I somehow missed that just acknowledging that I was a sinner and feeling guilt and shame wasn't the end. Romans 6:23 says, "For the wages of sin is death, but the gift of God is eternal life through Christ Jesus." I had memorized, as every VBS kid has, John 3:16: "For God so loved the world that He gave His one and only Son, that whoever believes in Him will not perish but have everlasting life." I knew Heaven and Hell were real places; I'm not sure I really realized that when my life on this earth was over, I would end up in one of those places. I'd memorized the Lord's Prayer—*Our Father in heaven…*—so when Josh said that Jesus said, "I am the way, the truth, and the life. No man comes to the Father except through Me," in John 14:6, some major dots started connecting.

I had completely missed Romans 10:9–10: "If you declare with your mouth, 'Jesus is Lord,' and believe in your heart that God raised Him from the dead, you will be saved. For it is with your heart that you believe and are justified, and it is with your mouth that you profess your faith and are saved." I mistakenly thought I needed to do good and be good to try to balance out the scales. Then he talked about the book of Ephesians, which I was admittedly not as familiar with. Chapter 2, verses 8 and 9 said, "For it is by grace you have been saved, through faith—and this is not from yourselves, it is a gift of God—not by works, so that no man can boast." *ROCKED!* I can't ever do enough to earn it.

As a result of Jesus' death on the cross for the payment of my sin and being raised to life, which demonstrates His power over death, I had a decision to make and an actual action to take. That belief required a confession with my mouth on my part, as Romans 10:9–10 says. I realized I was supposed to be reading the Bible and, as a result of what it said, acting on its commands (Jesus said, "If you love me, obey my commands"), allowing the Holy Spirit to change habits and begin conforming me to be like Christ.

I kind of felt like Azeem in the movie *Robin Hood* with Kevin Costner—I owed Jesus a life debt. He had paid for my life with His. Remember those group projects I'm not fond of? Well, the only way to get the A in this case is to surrender my own self-perceived merit, admit my faults (sins), and turn from them(repent)—and realize Jesus was doing ALL the work and turning it in. The "A" I was getting was the atonement for my sin, a debt that even if I was hung on a cross in the same way, I still couldn't pay because I don't meet the requirements of being without sin. Jesus is the only human ever to be able to do that—for all of us.

It was impossible to be like Christ if I didn't study Him. During that invitation, I stood—I couldn't have resisted if I tried. It felt as though I levitated up those steps to go talk to someone about what I had just realized. I confessed Jesus Christ as my Lord and Savior, which meant making Him Lord of my life in that everything I did from there on out needed to run through a filter of the Holy Spirit— which is quickly how Proverbs 3:5–6 became my go-to verses all those years ago.

I left that concert redeemed and forgiven, forever changed in an instant, but on a journey of daily being conformed to the image of Christ, which, according to Philippians 1:6, will continue until I die or Jesus comes back. I was baptized in a public profession of faith the following Sunday. Some days are better than others; some days I easily yield to the Holy Spirit, and others it is a battle I fail and have to pray for forgiveness.

If you've never had a moment where you put all these things together and realized you are a sinner in need of Jesus as your Savior, will you let today be the day? Will you pray a simple prayer out loud, calling upon the name of the Lord to be saved? Romans 10:13 says, "For all who call on the name of the Lord shall be saved." There's nothing special about your words—remember, Romans 10:9–10 says it has to do with the posture of your heart—that you declare with your mouth, "Jesus is Lord," and *believe* in your heart God raised Him from the dead; you will be saved.

If you've just prayed to receive salvation, let me be among the first to congratulate you and welcome you to the Church—the actual body of believers across the whole earth, not just a building where you go. Let me also encourage you to tell someone about the decision you just made! Let me encourage you to get a Bible and start reading, if its new for you I might recommend getting an NIV or NASB translation and maybe start in Matthew in the New Testament. And let me encourage you to join a local church body so you can deepen your understanding, be discipled, disciple others, and serve within the body of Christ.

About the Author

Raychel Shaw is an author, instructor, and storyteller with a passion for encouraging others through transparent, faith-filled writing. A graduate of Southwestern Baptist Theological Seminary and Stephen F. Austin (Axe'm Jacks). Drawing from her own seasons of change, challenge, and hope, she writes in a way that meets readers in the middle of their real-life struggles and points them toward the truth of God's Word.

She is the author of children's books I Love You This Much, I Love You This Much More, and If I Was a Squirrel for a Day, as well as a growing collection of devotionals and inspirational works. Whether through her books, blog, or speaking engagements, Raychel's heart is to help people tether themselves to the hope found in Jesus.

When she's not writing, you can find her enjoying coffee and tea, caring for her animals, or spending time with her family in East Texas. Connect with Raychel at www.RaychelWrites.com or on social media @RaychelWrites and shop her personally crafted coffee and tea collection at shopwritersraost.com.

www.ingramcontent.com/pod-product-compliance
Lightning Source LLC
Chambersburg PA
CBHW060815050426
42449CB00008B/1667